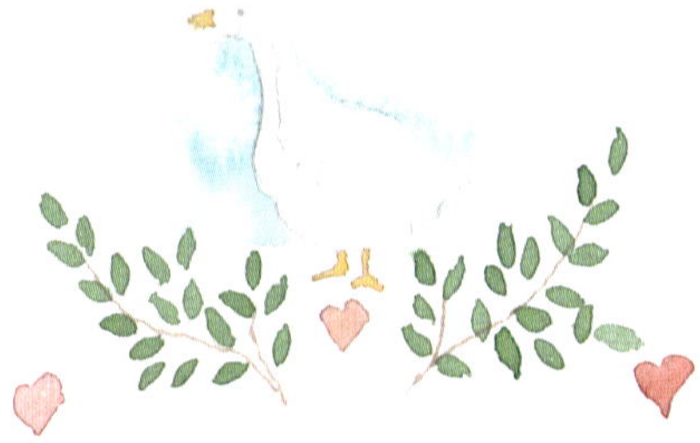

OUR NEW BABY

....

The information in this book is intended to be used to supplement rather than substitute the advice of a doctor. If you are concerned about the health or well-being of yourself or your baby, please consult your GP or paediatrician.

First published 1996 by Merehurst Limited,
Ferry House, 51-57 Lacy Road, London SW15 1PR

ISBN 1-85391-537-8

A catalogue record of this book is available from the British Library.

Designed by Hammond Hammond
Typesetting by Michael Weintroub/Hammond Hammond
Colour separation by Pixel Tech. Pte Ltd, Singapore
Printed in Hong Kong by Wing King Tong

OUR NEW BABY

Catherine O'Dolan

ILLUSTRATED BY
Nicola Gregory

MEREHURST

PREGNANCY NOTES

Mother's feelings when she discovered that she was pregnant:

Father's feelings:

Baby's due date:

Mother's feelings during pregnancy:

Father's feelings during pregnancy:

Any food cravings:

Favourite names for a boy:

Favourite names for a girl:

Attach scan photograph

BABY'S AGE AT SCAN:

....

DATE:

....

OUR BABY'S ARRIVAL

NAME:

....

DATE OF BIRTH: ....

TIME OF BIRTH: ....

WEIGHT: ....

LENGTH: ....

HAIR COLOUR:

....

NAME CHOSEN BY:

....

... BECAUSE:

....

....

Attach first photograph of baby

DATE:

....

THE BIRTH

Where the birth took place:

Labour lasted:

Pain relief:

Method of delivery:

Name of birth partner:

Name of doctor or midwife:

Comments about the birth:

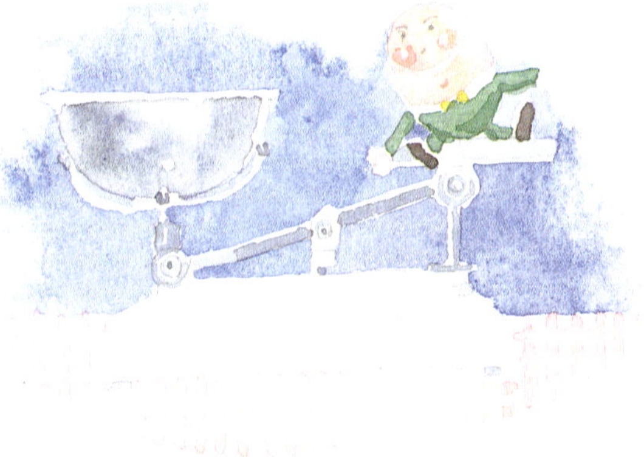

Attach any special mementoes, such as hospital bracelet, lock of hair, foot or handprint, birth plan

FIRST IMPRESSIONS

Our baby's appearance:

Any family resemblances:

The most surprising thing is:

Mother's first words after the birth:

Father's first words after the birth:

Mother's feelings after one week:

Father's feelings after one week:

MILESTONES AT BIRTH

Babies are born with some amazing reflexes. Most babies have a very strong grip – if you offer your baby a finger, she'll curl her fingers around it tightly and won't want to let go. This tight grip disappears after a couple of days, although your baby will still be able to hold objects such as a rattle if you place it in her hand.

A new-born baby can also make a 'stepping' motion if you hold her upright with her feet on a flat surface, although, of course, she can't walk or support her own weight. This 'stepping' reflex disappears during the early weeks.

Your baby can focus at a distance of around 10 inches (25 cm) in front of her. That's just the distance between your eyes and hers as you feed her.

Your baby's sucking reflex is usually highly developed too, although this may not be the case if your baby is born premature. Gently brush the corner of your baby's mouth with your finger and she'll turn towards it and open her mouth ready to suckle.

Your baby might have a mass of thick hair or be completely bald. Newborns often have little pink or red marks on their skin which fade gradually. Spots and rashes are common too and are usually no cause for concern. Her head might look an odd shape or appear to be slightly swollen. This could be due to pressure during the birth, or a forceps delivery. Your paediatrician or GP will examine your newborn to check her physical health and reflexes.

CURRENT EVENTS AT THE TIME OF OUR BABY'S BIRTH

Favourite musicians:

....

Top of the charts (album/single):

....

Film of the year:

....

Most popular actors:

....

Book of the year:

....

Sporting heroes:

....

Prime minister:

....

Political party:

....

News headlines:

....

Women's fashion:

....

Men's fashion:

....

Prices:

Loaf of bread

....

Pair of jeans

....

Baby stretchsuit

....

Pint of milk

....

Daily newspaper

....

Pack of nappies

....

Attach special mementoes, such as newspaper cuttings on baby's birthday, weather report, your baby's horoscope, current exchange rates

FIRST VISITORS

NAME: ....

REMARKS:

....

GIFT:

....

NAME: ....

REMARKS:

....

GIFT:

....

NAME: ....

REMARKS:

....

GIFT:

....

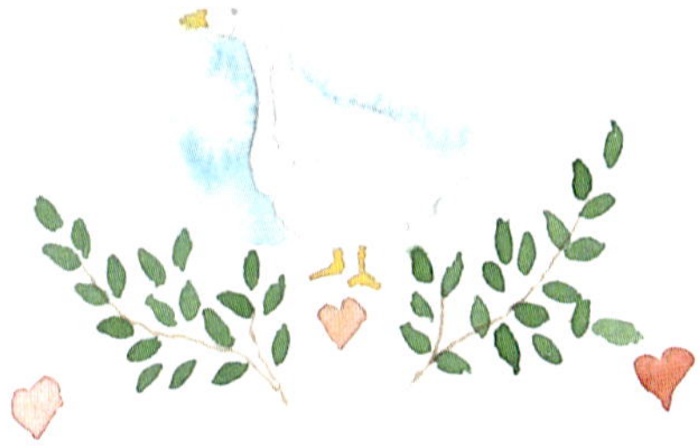

Attach mementoes such as congratulation cards and telegrams, or jot down any telephone messages

FAMILY TREE

Attach family photographs and caption each one with name and date of birth

BABY

....

....

MOTHER

....

....

GRANDMOTHER

GRANDFATHER

....

....

....

....

AUNTS AND UNCLES (ON MOTHER'S SIDE):

....

....

Brothers and Sisters

....

....

Father

....

....

Grandmother

Grandfather

....

....

Aunts and uncles (on father's side):

....

....

COMING HOME

Our address is:

....

....

Our baby came home on:

....

If the baby was born at home,
our first night on our own was:

....

Mother's feelings:

....

....

Father's feelings:

....

....

The first night was:

....

....

....

Attach photograph of
baby's first home,
nursery or bedroom

THE FIRST WEEKS

Starting your family life with a new baby is an exciting experience, but it's only natural to feel nervous and apprehensive about what's in store for you and your partner. You may feel overwhelmed by the sudden sense of responsibility for this tiny, helpless being, but you'll soon learn to cope, gaining confidence as the days and weeks pass and you become more accustomed to your new role as parents.

Take your lead from your baby. For the first few weeks he'll sleep between 8 and 16–20 hours a day, but usually only for 20–30 minutes at a time. His waking hours may be spent feeding, having his nappy changed and getting to know you and his new world.

Handle your baby with tender loving care, gently supporting his neck in the crook of your arm as you lift him, as he can't yet support his head. Always place his bottom down safely in his cot before releasing your hold. Babies have an inborn fear of falling and your baby may suddenly throw out his arms and legs if he thinks you are going to let him fall. But remember that babies are more robust and resilient than they look! If your baby seems alarmed, then he's simply letting you know that he wants you to be a little more gentle with him.

Babies can't regulate their own body temperature very well, so keep your baby's room at a constant temperature of around 65°F (18°C) or slightly warmer for the first couple of weeks. Use a nursery wall thermometer to check the temperature. Gently touch the back of your baby's neck or his tummy to check he's comfortable. If his skin feels sticky, he's too warm; if it feels very cold, he may be too chilly. Use layers of light clothing to cover your baby, so that you can remove or add layers easily.

You may be experiencing roller-coaster emotions – one minute you're exhilarated and delighted, the next you feel inexplicably down or burst into tears for no apparent reason. Many mums get the 'baby blues' a few days after the birth, often coinciding with their milk coming in which can cause some discomfort.

Make the most of the professionals who are there to help you. Your community midwife will probably visit for the first 10 days – discuss any queries or worries you have, but trust your own judgement and instincts too. You know your baby better than anyone else.

Be gentle with yourself. Giving birth is an exhausting physical task and you need rest to help you recover, especially if you've had a Caesarean or painful stitches. Make sure you attend your 6 week postnatal check to ensure that your body is returning to normal after the birth.

Try to get as much rest as possible. Nap when your baby does, rather than attempting to rush round doing household chores. It's not easy to get used to lack of sleep and being at the beck and call of a tiny baby. Put on the answerphone, if you have one, or take the phone off the hook when you don't want to be disturbed. Don't feel pressurised into having visitors if you don't feel up to it. Explain politely that you'd just like a little quiet time to yourselves.

There are a variety of ways to hold your baby. Try different positions to find the ones which are most comfortable for you. Let his head rest on your shoulder or on your chest, or rest his bottom on your hip, but always try to keep your back straight to avoid backache. Your baby will love being close to you where he can feel your warmth, and he'll be reassured by the sound of your heartbeat and breathing.

Relaxation is the key to surviving the early weeks, although it's easier said than done! But if you're stressed, your baby may sense this and become unsettled too.

Try to eat a healthy diet, especially if you're breastfeeding – plenty of fresh fruit and vegetables, pasta, cereals, lean meat and poultry, and drink lots of water. It's a good idea to start some gentle exercise to tone your body, including your daily pelvic floor exercises to strengthen muscles.

Don't forget to register your baby's birth within 6 weeks. You'll find your nearest Registry Office in the telephone directory, or ask your health visitor to advise you. If you're married, either you or your husband can register the birth. If not, your partner must be present when you register the birth if he wants to be named on the birth certificate.

APPEARANCE

	AT BIRTH	AT 6 MONTHS	AT 1 YEAR
HAIR:	....	....	....
EYES:	....	....	....
EYELASHES:	....	....	....
EYEBROWS:	....	....	....
COMPLEXION:	....	....	....
TEETH:	....	....	....
DISTINGUISHING FEATURES:	....	....	....

OVERALL APPEARANCE AT BIRTH:

....

....

OVERALL APPEARANCE AT 6 MONTHS:

....

....

OVERALL APPEARANCE AT 1 YEAR:

....

....

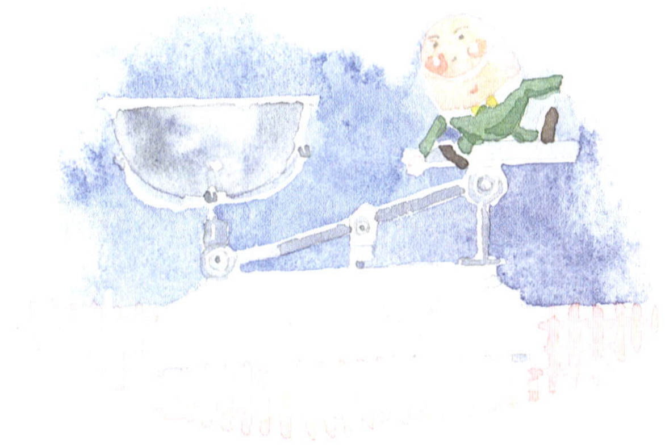

HEIGHT AND WEIGHT RECORD

	Weight	Height
At birth:	....	....
3 months:	....	....
6 months:	....	....
9 months:	....	....
1 year:	....	....
18 months:	....	....
2 years:	....	....

HEALTH RECORD

Immunisation

Immunisation is the most effective way to protect your baby against certain childhood diseases. Your baby is given (either by mouth or by injection) a tiny dose of the bacteria or virus which causes the disease, in order to help her to develop a natural immunity. It's important for your baby to have the full course of vaccines to ensure maximum protection. If you have any queries, ask your health visitor or GP for advice.

When due	Date of appointment	Immunisation	Method
2 months	....	Haemophilus influenzae type B (Hib) Diphtheria } Tetanus } DTP Pertussis (Whooping cough) } Polio	One injection One injection By mouth
3 months	....	Haemophilus influenzae type B (Hib) Diphtheria } Tetanus } DTP Pertussis (Whooping cough) } Polio	One injection One injection By mouth
4 months	....	Haemophilus influenzae type B (Hib) Diphtheria } Tetanus } DTP Pertussis (Whooping cough) } Polio	One injection One injection By mouth
12-15 months	....	Measles } Mumps } MMR Rubella }	One injection
3-5 years	....	Diphtheria } Tetanus } Polio	Booster injection By mouth

Development reviews

Your health visitor or GP will offer you regular appointments to check your baby's progress, health (including hearing and eyesight) and general behaviour.

Comments at 6-8 weeks:

....

....

....

Comments at 6-9 months:

....

....

....

Comments at 18-24 months:

....

....

....

Contact names and telephone numbers:

Doctor's name: ....

Telephone number: ....

Community midwife or health visitor: ....

Telephone number: ....

Baby clinic: ....

Telephone number: ....

Nearest Accident and Emergency Department:: ....

Telephone number: ....

FEEDING

Your baby needs nourishment to help her grow and develop, but feeding is much more than that – it's a time for closeness and affection between you and your baby. It's no coincidence that your newborn focuses at roughly 10 inches (25 cm), as this is the distance between your eyes and hers when she's feeding. The decision to breast or bottle feed is a personal one and only you can decide which is best for you and your baby. However, it is recommended that mums breastfeed for at least the first 4 months.

BREASTFEEDING

Breastfeeding has many benefits for you and your baby. Breastmilk contains all the vital nutrients your baby needs, it's convenient (no sterilising) and it's free. Breastfeeding also helps your uterus to contract to its normal size and many breastfeeding mums find that it helps them to regain their figure more quickly as well. Breastmilk may also help to protect your baby against certain infections and allergies.

Many mums experience some difficulties when they start breastfeeding, but don't feel disheartened. It takes time to learn any new skill, so try to persevere. In the meantime you need encouragement and support from those around you. Discuss your problems with your community midwife or ask to see a special breastfeeding counsellor (contact your local branch of the National Childbirth Trust for details).

Always seek advice or reassurance from your community midwife or health visitor if you have problems, such as sore or cracked nipples or a lump in your breast which may be a blocked duct. These are common difficulties which can often be resolved quickly with expert help.

It's important that your baby is properly latched onto the breast. If you stroke the corner of your baby's mouth with your finger, she'll open it ready to latch on. Look at the muscles at your baby's temples or see if her ears are wiggling while she sucks – this means she's latched on and feeding well! Her bottom lip should be curled down with her chin resting against your breast. When your baby has had enough milk, she'll stop sucking. Gently slide your finger in at the corner of her mouth to break the suction. Don't pull her straight off, as this will drag your nipple and may make it sore.

Drink plenty of fluids (water, fruit juice or milk), eat a healthy balanced diet and try to rest. This will help you to keep up with the 'supply and demand' – that is, the more your baby wants to feed, the more milk your breasts will provide.

Don't be tempted to substitute formula feeds if you think your breastfeeds are not satisfying your baby, as this can result in your breasts producing less milk. To encourage more milk, try expressing after a feed. Ask your midwife for advice if you're worried.

Use absorbent nursing pads and wear a well-fitting support bra which exposes one breast fully for feeding while the other breast is supported. Avoid using soap on your breasts as this may have a drying effect on the skin's natural lubrication.

BOTTLEFEEDING

One of the main benefits of bottlefeeding is that your partner can become more involved. He can also give your baby expressed breastmilk in a bottle.

Bottlefeeding requires more equipment than breastfeeding. You'll need at least six bottles and teats. Once you get into a routine you'll probably find it easier to mix several feeds at a time and store them in the fridge for up to 24 hours. All equipment must be sterilised to protect your baby against infection. There are several methods: cold water and sterilising tablets or liquid, or steam or microwave sterilisers which are quick and efficient.

All babies feed differently. Some may be content to feed every three to four hours; others may prefer 'little and often'. Your baby will let you know when she's had enough and won't always want to finish a whole bottle. Discard any milk that's left.

Whether your baby is breast or bottlefed, you can incorporate winding at the end of each feed (bottlefed babies tend to be more windy than breastfed babies). Sit your baby on your knee then rub or pat her back gently for a few minutes to release any excess wind, but don't expect your baby to produce a burp every time.

Some babies bring up a little milk after a feed. This is nothing to worry about, provided your baby is well and gaining weight. Ask your health visitor or GP if you're at all concerned.

KEEPING YOUR BABY CLEAN

Nappy Changing

By the time your baby is potty trained, you'll have changed his nappy around 5,000 times. At first he'll probably dirty his nappy around 6–8 times a day. As you become accustomed to your baby, you'll be able to tell when he's soiled his nappy: apart from the obvious smell, he may cry if he's uncomfortable or wet. Frequent nappy changes will also help to prevent soreness or nappy rash.

You can buy either disposable or washable nappies. Disposables are more convenient but also slightly more expensive. Reusable nappies are a more environmentally friendly option but mean a lot of washing; thicker shaped nappies also take a long time to dry. You could look for a nappy laundering service in your area, which will save you having to wash nappies yourself, although, of course, this will work out more expensive than washing your own.

It's worth investing in a plastic wipe-clean changing mat, although you can just as easily change your baby on a towel protected by a waterproof sheet. The safest place to change your baby is on the floor. If you use a changing table, make sure that you never leave your baby unattended, even for a moment.

Ensure that you have all you need for a quick change before you begin. You'll need cotton wool and warm water (cooled boiled water for a newborn) or baby lotion to cleanse your baby's bottom and genitals, a clean nappy, nappy cream (if using), and nappy pin, liner and plastic pants if you're using traditional washable nappies.

Wipe your baby girl's bottom from front to back, away from the vagina to prevent spreading germs. For boys, gently clean the tip of the penis, but don't pull back the foreskin. When changing a boy, hold the dirty nappy over his penis for a few seconds before removing. It's quite common for boys to sprinkle a pee when you remove their nappy.

Choose stretchsuits and leggings with poppers round the crotch and down both legs, so that you can undo the bottom half of your baby's outfit to change his nappy without him being completely naked.

Most babies get nappy rash at some time and their bottom becomes red or spotty. To ease soreness, change your baby's nappy more frequently and let him lie on a mat or towel without a nappy for a little while to let the air get to his skin and help it breathe. If the rash does not improve, check with your GP or health visitor that there is no infection, such as thrush.

Sometimes a baby can go for several days without passing a motion, especially if he's breastfed, but this doesn't mean he's constipated. If you're worried, mention it to your midwife or health visitor. Likewise, tell them if you're concerned about the contents of your baby's nappy, if your baby has diarrhoea or if his stools are very watery or smelly.

Topping and Tailing

Your newborn won't need a bath every day, but you should 'top and tail' him daily, carefully washing his 'top' half (face, neck, hands) and his 'tail' end (his bottom).

Gather everything you need before you begin and make sure that the room is warm and draught-free. Use warm water (boiled and cooled for a newborn) and cotton wool.

First clean your baby's face, neck and hands. Use a separate piece of cotton wool for each eye, gently wiping from the middle outwards towards his ears. Clean around your baby's ears, but there's no need to clean inside. Clean his bottom every time you change his nappy.

For a more thorough clean but without having a bath, sponge him down on his changing mat. If your baby doesn't like being naked, undo his top half first, then his bottom half. Use a sponge and warm water to wash his tummy while he's lying on his back, then pat him dry. Sit him up and wash his back, then pat dry. Wrap him in a soft, warm towel and give him a reassuring cuddle afterwards.

MILESTONES – THE FIRST FEW MONTHS

Record your baby's early development here. For example, by 3 months, she might be able to hold up her head, move her head from side to side and follow moving objects with her eyes.

AGE: SKILLS:

....

....

....

....

....

RECOGNISES MOTHER AT: ....

RECOGNISES FATHER AT: ....

FIRST SMILE AT: ....

FIRST GIGGLE AT: ....

BABY SLEEPS FOR: ....

BEST WAY TO SOOTHE YOUR BABY: ....

....

FAVOURITE GAMES OR PASTIMES: ....

....

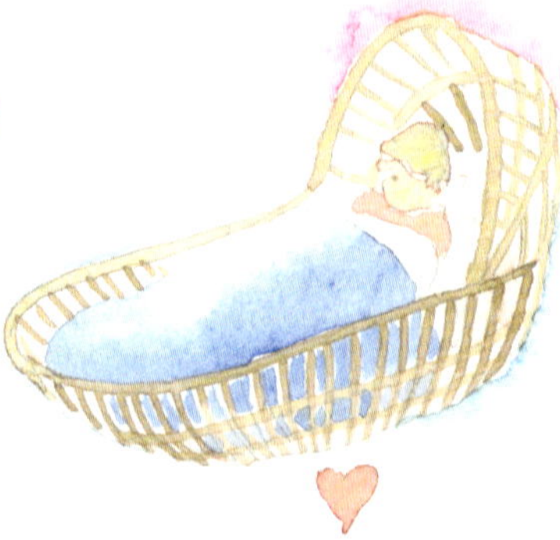

BABY'S PERSONALITY: ....

....

ANY PET NAMES THAT YOU CALL YOUR BABY: ....

....

BECAUSE: ....

....

....

Attach photographs of your baby at 2–3 months

CRYING

As you get to know your baby, you'll soon begin to be able to interpret what her different cries mean – she may be hungry, have a dirty nappy or be overtired; she may want a little companionship or just want to be held close with a cuddle. Always see to your baby's need as soon as possible; pick her up and rock her gently to try to soothe her. In the early months the best way to settle her is usually to feed her.

Young babies do most of their crying in the first three months, when they cry an average of two hours a day, although all babies are different and some cry more than others.

If your baby likes to be held close most of the time, you may find it more convenient to use a baby sling so that you can carry your baby and still get on with other chores at the same time. Some babies also find the steady whirring of the vacuum cleaner or the washing machine soothing!

Babies can get bored, so provide some simple entertainment. Once your baby can support her head, she may enjoy sitting in a bouncing chair and watching the world go by. Position her where she can gaze out of the window (but make sure she's not in a draught) or place a mobile or colourful picture nearby for her to look at. Never place a bouncing chair on a table or raised surface, and don't leave her unattended.

If your baby is crying inconsolably and you can't seem to appease her, a change of scene may do the trick. Take her for a walk in the pram or for a short drive.

From 6 months, your baby may cry when she's separated from you. Let her get to know new faces while you're around to reassure her.

If your baby cries often in the early evening with a sharp piercing cry, drawing her knees up to her chest, she may have colic. Unfortunately there is no simple cure for colic, although you can try to soothe her in the usual way by rocking her, singing or talking to her softly, or stroking her gently. If crying persists, ask your GP or health visitor for advice.

SLEEP

Your newborn baby will probably spend most of the day asleep – up to 16–20 hours a day, but in short bursts of about 20 minutes at a time. Occasionally he may wake up and cry but drift peacefully off to sleep again after a short feed.

Always place your baby on his back (or side) to sleep, unless your doctor advises you otherwise for medical reasons; if he is placed on his side, rest your baby's arm out in front of him to prevent him from rolling over.

Your baby will sleep anywhere, as long as he's warm and comfortable. You can use a cot or moses basket, carry-cot or baby car seat for short naps. Normal household noise will not disturb your baby. It's better for your baby to get used to sleeping with a certain amount of noise, otherwise you may find he'll only sleep when it's completely quiet.

Use light bedding, such as a sheet and cellular blanket. Duvet and cot bumpers are not recommended for babies under 12 months, due to the risk of overheating, and do not use pillows. Make sure that your baby cannot be covered completely by bedclothes. The covers should reach no further than his shoulders.

By 3 months, your baby will be awake for longer during the day, but he will probably still wake 3 or 4 times during the night. By 6 months, your baby will start to sleep longer at night, and hopefully a clear day and night pattern will begin to emerge.

Try to establish different day and night routines. Nappy changing and daytime feeds can be more lively and animated; at night, keep them low key and quiet with dim subdued lighting and put your baby straight back to bed after seeing to his needs.

FIRST CELEBRATION

We held a celebration for our baby on:

....

At:

....

Baby's age:

....

Details of ceremony
(such as christening, baptism or naming):

....

....

Baby's outfit:

....

....

Baby's reaction:

....

....

Guests:

....

....

....

....

....

Attach celebration photographs or special mementoes, such as invitations, cards or Order of Service cards

FIRST OUTINGS

The first time we left the house, we went to:

Date:

Travelled by:

Baby's reaction:

Other memorable early outings – for example, a visit to the park, to grandparents, to the mother and toddler group or the swimming pool:

Place:

Date:

Baby's reaction:

Place:

Date:

Baby's reaction:

Attach photographs of days out – write place and date underneath – or attach other mementoes, such as ticket stubs

GETTING OUT AND ABOUT

It's good for you and your baby to get out of the house once a day to get some fresh air and a change of scenery. It's also a great way to get some exercise and meet other parents for a chat.

If you plan to go shopping or travel on public transport, avoid the rush hour. Opt for less crowded times such as mid-morning or mid-afternoon rather than busy lunchtimes.

Make sure that your baby is properly dressed for the weather. Wrap her up warmly in winter and make sure that she's wearing a hat, as most body heat is lost through the head. But remove extra layers when you come indoors to avoid overheating.

Babies under 6 months should always be kept out of direct sunlight. In summer, apply a sun lotion with a high sun protection factor (SPF) or sunblock to protect your baby's delicate skin. Encourage her to wear a wide-brimmed hat and use a sun canopy on your pram. Attach window blinds for long car journeys to keep her in the shade.

Whenever you travel by car, your baby must be safely secured in a rear-facing car seat. If the passenger seat has an airbag, the car seat must be attached in the back seat (still rear-facing). Many parents find an infant carrier with a handle is convenient as a first stage car seat.

If you find your pram a bit bulky to manoeuvre, especially when you're out on your own or using public transport, try carrying your baby in a sling. Your baby will love to be close to you and it leaves both your hands free too. When your baby can sit up confidently on her own, she may prefer an over-the-shoulder carrier which gives her a better view.

WHAT TO PACK

Gone are the days when you could dash out of the house at a moment's notice. Whenever you go out with your baby, you need a certain amount of paraphernalia. But don't worry – if you keep a bag of essentials ready packed, you can still make a relatively speedy getaway. Here are some of the basic items which you'll need for early outings with your baby:

A changing bag with an integral changing mat. Choose one with plenty of pockets and compartments for storage.

A couple of disposable nappies. Even if you use washable nappies, you'll find disposables infinitely more convenient than carrying a soiled nappy in your bag.

Baby wipes (handy for cleaning bottoms as well as wiping sticky fingers or dirty faces), nappy cream, nappy sacks and any other essentials for changing your baby's nappy. Look for special mini travel packs (refillable if possible) or trial size packs for convenience.

Favourite toys, soother or small book to amuse your baby.

Feeding equipment - bottle and baby food, eating utensils such as spoon and bib. If you're worried about breastfeeding in public, wear a front-opening garment and take a shawl or scarf that you can drape loosely around yourself and your baby for discreet feeds.

Camera, film and batteries - you don't want to miss any special photo opportunities when you're out!

BATHTIME

When your baby is tiny, there's no need to give him a bath every day – a 'top and tail' wash is sufficient. However, you'll want to give him a bath a couple of times a week. You may feel nervous the first few times but, as with all the other new skills you're learning now, you'll soon be proficient.

You can buy a baby bath, use a washing up bowl or put your baby in the full-sized bath. If you prefer, have a bath with your baby, although it's safer when someone else is on hand to help by passing your baby to you and taking him out afterwards.

Babies can't regulate their temperature very well, so, when bathing your baby, make sure that the room is warm and free from draughts. The bath water should be warm but not hot, and you only need a couple of inches. Use your elbow or wrist to test the water temperature or use a bath thermometer.

Make sure you have everything you need before you put your baby in the bath. Never leave your baby unattended in the bath, even for a second.

Lower your baby gently into the bath, with your forearm supporting behind his back and your hand under his arm so that his head is resting in the crook of your arm; place your other hand under his bottom as you ease him in. Use this hand to trickle warm water gently from the bath over his body, while still supporting him with your other arm. Use a mild soap or gentle baby bath liquid to cleanse and moisturise your baby's skin.

Some babies instantly love the water, kicking and splashing happily. Others may cry. If your baby doesn't like it, he may prefer to bath with you or your partner to hold and reassure him until he's more confident.

Invest in a few bath toys to make bathtime fun – a sailing boat, floating duck or sponge bath book, or use household items such as a plastic jug or small watering can for pouring and splashing games.

To wash your baby's hair, use a brush with very soft bristles and a small amount of gentle shampoo. Rinse thoroughly with clean warm water, using a damp cloth or sponge. If your baby doesn't like having his hair washed, use a special shampoo shield – a bit like a wide brimmed hat with an open top which is designed to keep the water away from his eyes.

After his bath wrap your baby in a soft, thick towel immediately. Gently pat dry, especially in the creases and folds of his skin. There's no need to use baby talcum powder. If you do want to, use only a very small amount. Shake it onto your hands first then rub your hands together before smoothing over your baby. Avoid shaking powder directly on to your baby as he may swallow dust particles.

Attach bathtime photograph

WEANING

Your baby will be ready for her first tastes of solid food from around 4–6 months. There's no rush to get your baby started on solids, she will let you know when she's ready. You may notice that she still seems hungry after a feed, starts to suck her fists, or even looks longingly at your food or tries to grab it! Your baby also needs to be able to sit up well as you feed her.

Milk will still be your baby's main food, but you can start with just a teaspoon or so of baby rice (preferably gluten free) mixed with breast or formula milk to make it smooth and runny.

Give your baby half of her usual breast or formula feed to take the edge off her hunger before you give her a spoonful of baby rice, then let her finish the rest of her usual feed. Let the rice slide off the spoon into your baby's mouth – don't try to push food to the back of your baby's mouth as she may splutter or choke. Your baby may turn up her nose at first – it's quite a change from what she's used to – so be patient.

Continue to give your baby a few spoonfuls of baby rice for a couple of weeks, gradually increasing the amount according to her appetite. Once she is eating a small portion of baby rice confidently, you can start to introduce new tastes like puréed, well cooked fruit and vegetables at a second feed, again starting with half her usual feed then a couple of spoonfuls of purée, followed by the rest of her feed.

After a few months your baby will be getting more used to taking mouthfuls of food and learning to chew. Now you can introduce slightly lumpier foods which can simply be mashed rather than puréed. Gradually increase the amount and variety of foods including lean, well-cooked meat, poultry and fish, and reduce her milk feeds.

Your baby will be working towards eating a wide variety of different food and having three small meals a day, with snacks in between, but as her stomach is tiny, she'll only be eating mini portions.

Whole cow's milk can be used in sauces or homemade custard or mixed with cereals from 6 months, but it is not suitable as a main drink until your baby is over 1 year old. If your baby is thirsty between feeds, offer her cooled boiled water from a trainer beaker, rather than fruit or herbal drinks, which often contain sugar and may encourage your baby to develop a sweet tooth and contribute towards tooth decay. Never add sugar or salt to your baby's food.

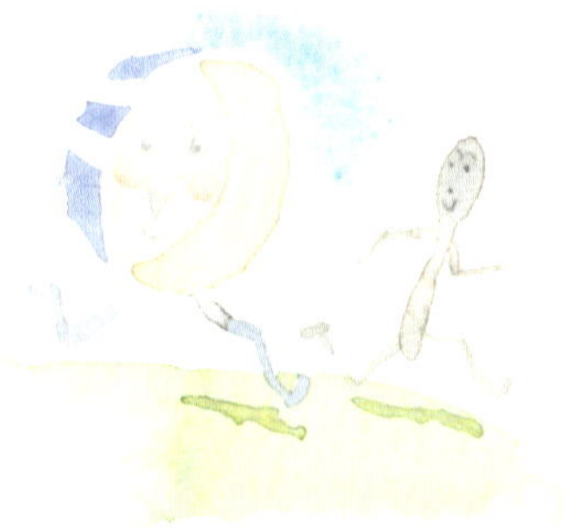

Our baby's first tastes of solids:

....

Our baby's favourite weaning food:

....

The first time our baby sat
in a highchair:

....

The first time our baby
held a spoon:

....

Attach mealtime photograph

PLAYTIME

Your newborn baby doesn't need toys to entertain her – she's quite happy to study the contours of your smiling face and slowly get accustomed to her new world. But once her neck muscles become stronger and she can hold up her head, her eyesight improves and she is more alert, she'll be ready to play....

——— · ———

From around 2 months, your baby will enjoy looking at bright objects in bold designs: hang a colourful mobile above her cot or let her lie under a baby gym which she can admire from below.

——— · ———

There's no need to buy lots of expensive toys – try making your own simple mobile by tying a piece of string across the bars of her cot and attach assorted items, such as empty cotton reels, jangling keys, strips of shiny paper or soft cotton wool, using bulldog clips or clothes peg to fasten them. (Make sure that your baby cannot pull down the string and remove the mobile as soon as she can sit up and grab it.) When your baby becomes bored, simply attach a new assortment.

——— · ———

Babies love repetition, so be prepared to repeat a favourite activity time and time again. Long before she can work out how to put one brick on top of another, she'll love to watch you build a tower for her to knock down again. Then wait for you to do it all over again!

——— · ———

Give her one toy at a time to play with. Babies can become over-stimulated or excitable if there's too much going on around them.

——— · ———

Most toys will have a recommended age range on the packaging; always buy toys for the appropriate age range and check that they conform to safety standards.

——— · ———

It's never too soon to introduce your baby to books. The most suitable are those with bold, bright pictures with easily recognisable everyday objects (such as animals or vehicles) or simple stories about familiar daily events, such as bathtime or shopping. Board books, soft cloth books and waterproof sponge books for bathtime are fun too.

Attach playtime photograph

Baby's favourite games:

....

Favourite toys:

....

Mother's favourite activities:

....

....

Father's favourite activities:

....

....

MILESTONES AT SIX MONTHS

All babies develop at different rates and your baby will go at his own pace. Remember, if your baby was born early, he'll probably reach his milestones later than he would if he was born at full term. If you are at all worried about your baby's rate of development, always contact your GP or health visitor for reassurance and advice. Here's a rough guide to some of the skills your baby will probably be developing when he reaches his half birthday:

He'll be able to support his head and turn it from side to side as he begins to observe the world around him.

He can support his weight on his forearms when lying on his stomach, almost as if he's doing a mini press-up, but only for a few seconds before he collapses in a heap!

He is able to sit up when he's well supported or propped up by cushions - he's gradually learning to sit up on his own, although he'll still lose his balance occasionally and topple over.

He'll make cooing noises and begin to chatter away in repetitive 'gagaga' sounds - he's experimenting with his voice, but only in his own unintelligible language.

He can reach out for and hold objects, but he's still hamfisted and tends to hold them in the palm of his hand rather than with his fingers. He probably likes to explore shapes and textures by putting objects in his mouth to suck them.

His vision is greatly improved and he can now focus across a room - and his face will light up when he recognises familiar faces, like his mummy and daddy.

Your baby's first tooth will probably appear around this time or in the next few months. Teething can cause discomfort and your baby may be grizzly, cry if you accidentally touch his sore gums and dribble more. A cool teether may ease pain, or give him a dry crust or a washed, peeled carrot to suck on.

Attach photograph of baby
aged 6 months

WHAT OUR BABY IS LIKE AT 6 MONTHS:

TYPICAL DAY FOR OUR BABY AT 6 MONTHS:

FIRST SUMMER

YEAR: ....

OUR BABY'S FAVOURITE OUTDOOR ACTIVITIES:

....

....

FAVOURITE OUTFIT:

....

FIRST TIME IN PADDLING POOL:

....

Attach photograph of
first summer here

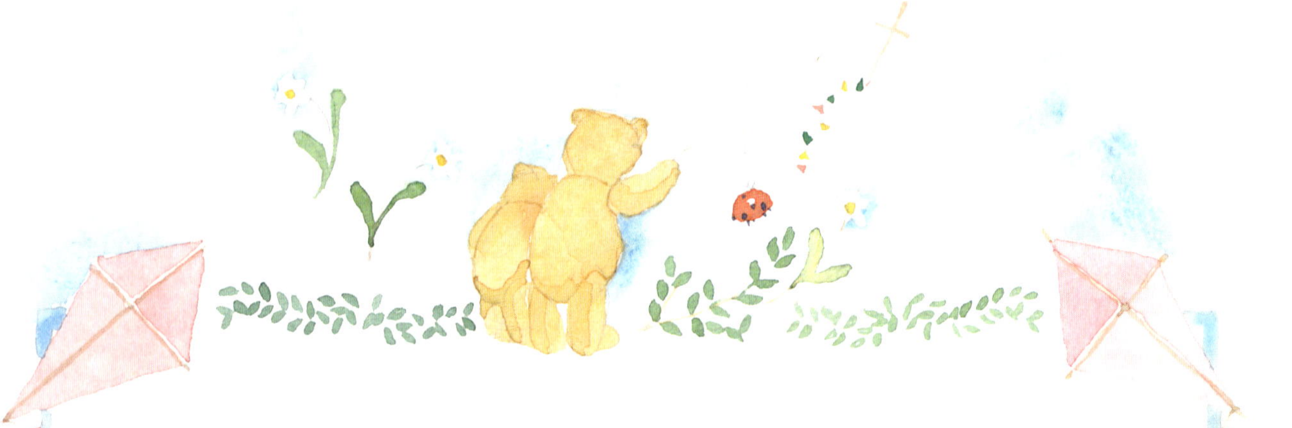

SPECIAL SUMMER EXCURSIONS

PLACE:

DATE:

BABY'S REACTION:

PLACE:

DATE:

BABY'S REACTION:

HANDS AND FEET

Your baby's tiny yet perfectly formed fingers and toes are one of her cutest features. They are also vital components in helping her to master some very important skills – handling objects and learning to walk.

As your baby becomes aware of her hands and feet, she'll find them fascinating, first to look at and then to put in her mouth. Many babies are so supple that they can suck their own toes with ease!

Your baby will enjoy 'supporting' her own weight on her legs if you bounce her up and down on your knee. Hold her gently under the arms or around her waist to support her as she bobs.

Your baby may also enjoy the sensation of a bouncer which you can hang in a doorway. However, don't use this for long periods of time as it may encourage her to point her toes, which could cause difficulties when she's learning to walk.

Check that your baby's socks and stretchsuits are sufficiently roomy around her toes. Babies' feet are soft and pliable, and can easily become misshapen if the feet are restricted. If stretchsuits become tight around the toes, cut off the foot section and use socks instead. There's no rush to buy your baby's first pair of shoes. She won't need them until she's walking outdoors. Until then barefoot is best.

Attach photograph of your baby on the move for the first time or hand and foot prints

From around 6–9 months your baby will be eager to be on the move. Give her lots of opportunity and space when she's learning to crawl. She'll start with mini press-ups, then lift her bottom and rock to and fro on her hands and feet until she finally moves off – often propelling herself backwards or shuffling along on her bottom.

To encourage your baby, hold a favourite toy just out of her reach. Give her plenty of praise when she manages to make her first move.

As your baby becomes mobile and ever more inquisitive, check that your home is safe. Move any breakable or hazardous objects out of reach, cover any electrical sockets and put round 'safety' corners on sharp edged tables or cupboards. Cover any glass doors with safety film. If you have an open fire, make sure that there is always a fireguard in front of it. A safety stairgate is also a worthwhile investment to ensure your curious explorer doesn't attempt to negotiate the stairs. Poisons (such as bleach), alcohol and medicines must be moved out of reach or locked away in cupboards.

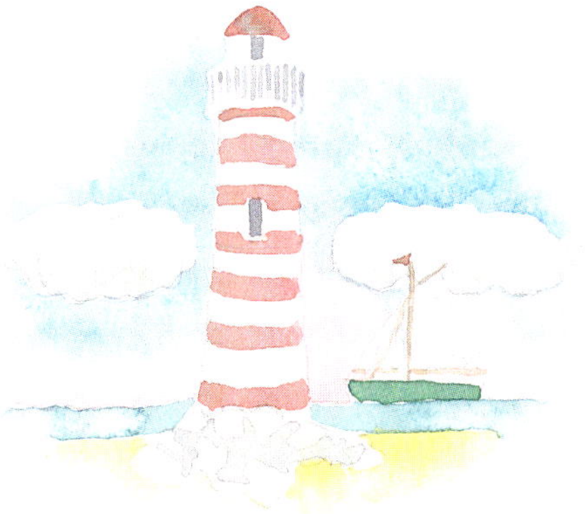

FIRST HOLIDAY

Date:

Baby's age:

Destination:

Duration of stay:

Travelled by:

Weather:

First time baby stood on the sand:

Baby's reaction:

First time baby paddled in the sea:

Baby's reaction:

Other holiday activities:

Attach photographs of baby's first holiday here

FIRST CHRISTMAS

Year: ....

Baby's age: ....

Christmas spent at:

....

with:

....

....

Weather on Christmas day:

....

Number 1 song at Christmas:

....

Baby's outfit:

....

Presents for baby:

....

....

Baby's first Christmas dinner:

....

....

Baby's reaction:

....

....

Mother's feelings:

....

....

Father's feelings:

....

....

Attach photograph of first Christmas here

MILESTONES AT 12 MONTHS

Your baby has come a long way in the past year and has achieved a great deal. Here's a rough guide to some of the skills your baby might have acquired by now (although of course all babies develop at their own rate). As he practises to perfect his many new skills, offer lots of encouragement along the way and give him enthusiastic praise for each one that he masters.

He'll babble constantly and might be able to say one or two words.

He'll probably understand 'No' - and might stop what he's doing and look at you for a minute, but he won't necessarily obey!

He can crawl at great speed or bottom shuffle to get to his destination, use furniture to cruise the room or maybe take a few unsteady steps on his own.

He may be able to stand unaided - albeit for a split second - or love to toddle with your support.

He loves to point and wave goodbye - at every opportunity. He'll also begin to recognise everyday objects that he sees in picture books and will enjoy pointing out familiar ones.

He can pick up small objects with dexterity using his thumb and forefinger, although he may still need assistance and encouragement from you.

DATES TO REMEMBER

Our baby's first tooth came through at:

....

Turned head from side to side at:

....

Lifted head when lying on stomach at:

....

Held head up at:	Made babbling noises at:
....	....
Played with hands at:	Played with feet at:
....	....
Held toys at:	Reached for objects at:
....	....

Rolled from tummy to back at:

....

Rolled from back to tummy at:

....

Passed object from one hand to another at:

....

Sat unsupported at:	Crawled at:
....	....
Stood unsupported at:	First tentative step at:
....	....

FIRST BIRTHDAY

How the day was celebrated:

....

Main present:..

First birthday cake:..

Mother's feelings looking back over the past year:

....

....

The best moment was: ....

The worst moment was: ....

Father's feelings looking back over the past year:

....

....

The best moment was: ....

The worst moment was: ....

Attach birthday photographs or mementoes such as cards

MAJOR DEVELOPMENTS

BABY'S AGE: ....

FAVOURITE GAMES: ....

....

FAVOURITE SONGS OR RHYMES: ....

....

FAVOURITE TOYS: ....

....

FAVOURITE BOOKS: ....

....

BEST FRIENDS: ....

....

FIRST WORD WAS: ....

...WHICH MEANS: ....

FAVOURITE WORDS: ....

...WHICH MEAN: ....

....

FIRST STEPS AT: ....

FIRST PAIR OF SHOES AT: ....

First time our baby danced: ....

...to (song): ....

First swim: ....

First time at playgroup: ....

First haircut: ....

Other memorable moments were: ....

....

....

....

Attach photographs of key developments, such as first steps or first haircut (take 'before' and 'after' photographs), or attach a lock of hair

SECOND BIRTHDAY

HOW THE DAY WAS CELEBRATED:

....

BABY'S OUTFIT:

....

MAIN PRESENT:

....

BIRTHDAY CAKE:

....

GUESTS:

....

....

....

....

BABY'S REACTION TO THE DAY:

....

....

....

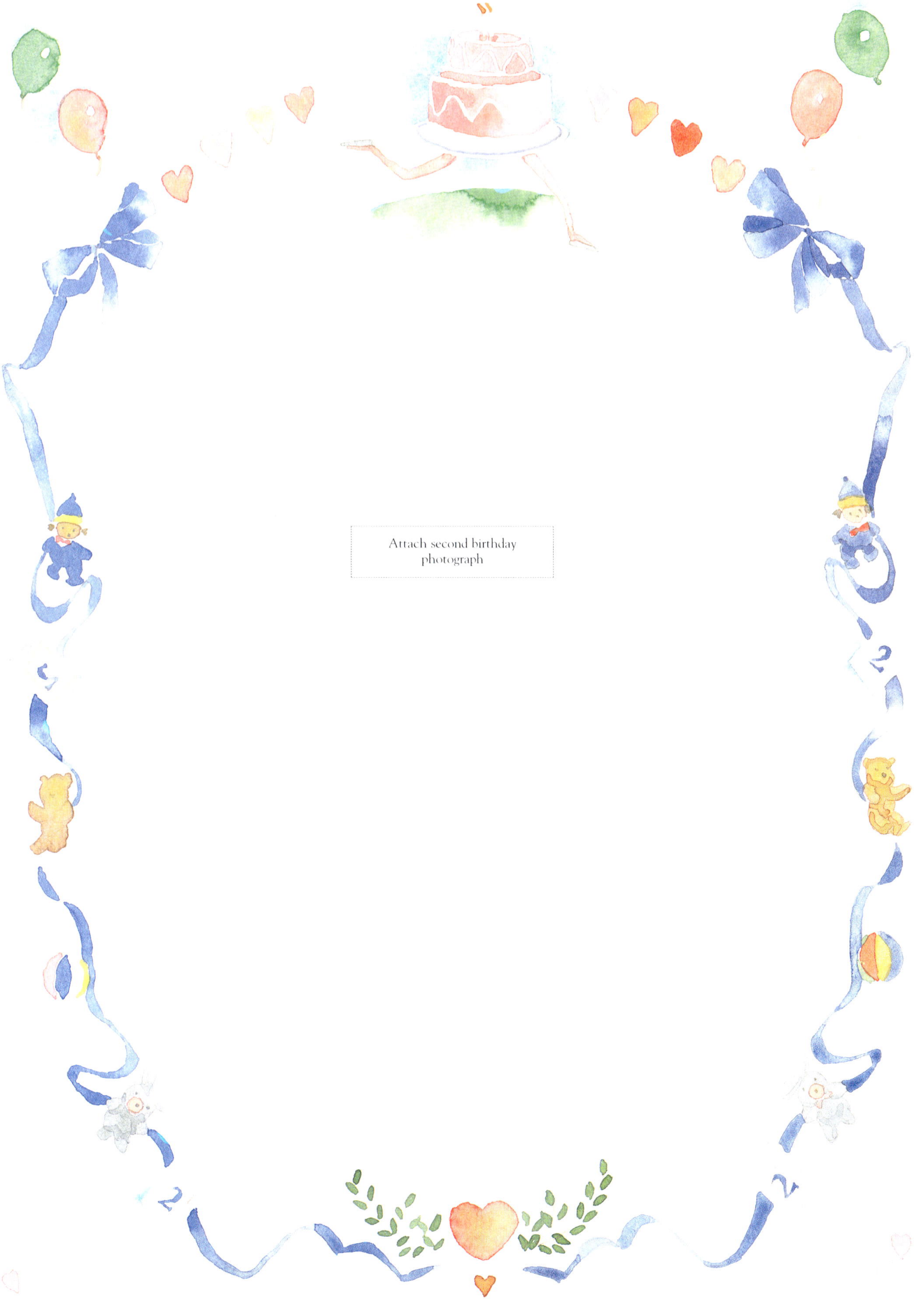

Attach second birthday photograph

PARENTS' IMPRESSIONS OF FIRST TWO YEARS

MOTHER'S FEELINGS:

THE BEST MOMENT WAS:

THE WORST MOMENT WAS:

FATHER'S FEELINGS:

THE BEST MOMENT WAS:

THE WORST MOMENT WAS: